Those Who Hold Up the Earth

Those Who Hold Up the Earth

Poems by

Peter F. Crowley

Cover design by Shay Culligan:

Cover art by Greg Orfanos

ISBN: 978-1-950462-97-1

Kelsay Books Inc.

kelsaybooks.com

502 S 1040 E, A119
American Fork,Utah 84003

This book is dedicated to my wife, Priyanka, family and friends. Specifically, to Priyanka who listened patiently and offered constructive feedback as I read these poems aloud to her on countless mornings and nights. To my friends Dan Morse, Linda Werbner and Stephen Waldron, who I've shared some of these pieces with, in an informal writers' group, and provided me with invaluable input. To my parents, Dave and Mary, who have always provided me with love and support, no matter what.

The soul of this book is dedicated to those who struggle to get by and who struggle for human dignity in the face of overwhelming odds. Perhaps most importantly, it is dedicated to those who are forgotten and taken for granted, who uphold the earth.

Acknowledgments

Boston Literary Magazine: "The Eternally Recurring Court of Memory"

The Opiate Literary Magazine: "Worker, Beg Not," "Mother Daughter Fight," "Freedom's not free," "Status threat," "Lit Crit"

Dissident Voice: "White Terrorist"

The Wilderness House Literary Review: "Onset of Fall," "The Wake"

Visitant: "Those who hold up the earth," "What we know, we already know"

WINK: Writers in the Know: "Time's recurrence and vanishing"

Work Literary Magazine: "All for the best"

The Improv 2008 Anthology of Colorado Poets: Peace, War, Love: "Merge," "After Awakening from Briar Patch Dreams"

Rhinocerotic: "Mudsill Populist"

Contents

Those who hold up the earth

There are people who hold up the earth.
With raised, soil-drenched arms held high
and herniated disks, they are weary,
their gaze diminished by the underground's thick, dark haze

Are they rickshaw puller
or did they pave the road he rides upon?
Are they dishwasher, with the stink of
sodden food permeating wrinkled hands?

Sometimes, when the world grows more weighty,
when teeth rip open the stomach of dreams and
the outside is dispossessed of any allure,
the ground they hold forces them to hunch over,
their backs nearly breaking.
But, somehow, they still manage to hold up the earth

What we know, we already know

They ate October for lunch,
wiped their lips with handkerchief
and drew a map of the world

Ginsburg's Gog and Magog
haunted mirrors' forgotten gaze
and ate salad as an afterthought

What we know, we already know
What we know, we already know
We already know what we know

It is imperishable, like the taste of
guava on a Dhaka morning
with heat on the seat
and war on the roads
It doesn't break down from tiny
black hole slices in the mirror's gulping Adam's apple,
nor from the stinking, putrid odor of truth.
It will tell us where we are on GPS
even if we lurk in a city fathoms away

And when we say that we'll live forever,
Gog and Magog clap, not without a hint of irony,
behind the marauding theater curtain
drawn during a restless sleep

Onset of Fall

As the breeze pours and purrs
by moving 1890s vehicle
and rises through hair and body
as though being were invisible
and appearance a transient moment

The dry cool air
brings together scattered pockets of early
wizened fallen leaves—a presage
of plant life's seasonal decay...
The onset of Fall invades the air

But the ocean waves
that crash you into the sand,
causing bathing suit pockets to fill up with it,
in which tiny mole crabs crawl...
This ocean, driven by wind in a mild Fury,
hurricane-aftershock...

This ocean
Still feels like summer

The Wake

Sitting on either side
The war now over

He looks glumly ahead,
a blank stare towards the coffin,
with fresh flowers surrounding—
tricking death with irony—
and muses on the broken bond of siblings.

There was nothing else he would've done,
so he shrugs at the impossibility of acting otherwise.
Then he talks to someone who came in and barely knew his sister
about a new business which drives people out 3 miles
where ashes can be legally thrown into international waters.
He chuckles when recounting people throwing ashes on a beach
and getting their wife or relative's altered chemical composition
blown back into the face

Meanwhile the dead woman's immediate elective family,
on the other side of the crowded visitation room,
shoot occasional glares in his direction

Through their mourning, they are held tight to an
adamant hatred against him

Maybe the war is not over...
And in a coffin, his sister lays before him,
waiting to become ash

The Eternally Recurring Court of Memory

Midnight's hands swelled
The cook lay her forehead down

Arcane eyelids drooped
Lavender time would again
sit upon forlorn pigeon stoops
dancing on the foam atop a beer

But now midnight drank a summation
to the eternally recurring court of fastidious memory...

Each pimple popped with zealous sadism
Each gossamer movie watched with horizontal lens
Each dinner cooked with brusque, McDonald's frying pan hands
Each morning with a sleeping body whispering good-bye
Each walk in the woods, with cameras seeking to elevate memory
Each argument resolved through dissipated hourglasses
Each embrace, recalling the wonders of flesh
that negates existentialism
Each marriage beg to linger over drunken cauldrons,
foretelling of alternate worlds in which time went backward, and
the spoon wooed a fork to test a betrothal soup
Each car ride to an event with anxious eyes and knowing smiles
Each caress with its cosmic plate of esteemed sunflowers
Each mirror nullifying the reflection of the person
standing next to you
Each menstrual glare of biological disillusionment
seeking chocolate
Each Valentine arrow that missed its collaborator,
flying over the shoulder
Each laugh untested by time

Each vessel lost at sea
Each note I ever played on the guitar for you spoke only for today
but you always sought tomorrow's song
Two dreams called self-perception could not remain juxtaposed
Each day they tried,
but all in vain

Worker, Beg Not

I.

Supplicated hands, extending
the beggar waits forever

From inside the glass office looking out,
such is the natural state of things

Make them wait, make them grovel,
have them kiss your feet
and one or two may be chosen
to ascend from the paycheck-to-paycheck
world to a place where one can
buy a newer car, which doesn't shake
you to the core as it ambles over bumps,
where one can hire a plumber
without a blink
where one can have a child
without ending up in the poorhouse

II.

What if we didn't care anymore
What if we said we'd no longer beg
What if the worker, no longer isolated in cubicle,
decided to lock arms
What if we all left at once
How, then, the headless coprophagic patients would scramble!
But, even then the scabs wouldn't be good enough
Those in the glass office would have to come
to terms with our demands
Just maybe we'd then have the funds for a child
or to purchase a newer car without going broke

Time

I.

We run through time, its ghosts, its arrows and its wings
Sometimes in the mornings, it becomes a damp cloth around
our mouths and nostrils
Its stare, that of an aardvark cornered by a hunter

Our gowns and flannels lose their color and the skin grows pallor
People die and we visit them, holding their hands while still warm
We look into the eyes of a wife who has lost her husband of
30 years, behind the tears there is a sense of an impending
void, the H of the H20 has been set adrift into a funeral pyre
Then we drink more heavily, swollen by evasive memories, and
ruminate upon our own death

II.

We run through time,
and nostalgia sometimes eats away at our core
Meadows of ancient open-endedness, where fertility lurked
in hyacinths and perennials' burgeoning stares to the azure
And where open windows breathed in the smells of autumn—
The comfort of wood-burning stoves and decaying brittle brown
leaves…how decay used to be romanticized in our young
existential minds that we, so removed from death,
feigned courage at supposedly facing it directly.
But, as the hourglass's sand pours towards us as would a tidal
wave, we stand like a frozen cadaver
resigned to the inevitable future of the decomposing autumnal leaf

III.

We run through time; its faces grow wrinkled and weary
Alas, there is no return to the 21-year old's intensity of
gloom, desire and sense of self.
We get older and often pretend not to:
    We muse on dating young, beautiful women as single men in
    our late 40s—if we were our younger selves, oh, how we would
    laugh!
    We cover our balding heads with trusty hats
    or abysmally-shaved skulls
    We obscure our graying beards with black dye that
    doesn't quite match the color of our hair.
    We have surgeons lift our faces and necks to fool others into
    perceiving us as younger than we are

    But we're fooling no one, least of all ourselves.

Time's Recurrence and Vanishing

An effervescent epoxy
sits on tawdry shelves,
in void environs of absence

With a click of the heels,
fairies emerge from Yeats' brain,
dwelling in northwest
Ireland's coastal mist,
'neath skies that turn
from sun-gazing fields of
sheep meadow
to abrupt maelstrom rains
that soon again yield azure

The fairies perform a céilí dance around the sleeper's head.
The sleeper, head resting on recurrent pillow,
dreams of imbibing liquid coal
from a tornado-shaped funnel.

Meanwhile, the dead, in their closed-eye, deep-soil stare,
provide feed for beetles and maggots, while their
hydroxyapatite dust fuels soil fecundity.
The amorphous fairies leap from hillside to hillside,
yielding farrow in the dead's moon-shadowed wake.

In turn, farrow is raised by keepers of the land,
the agriculturalists, who rear them to a ripe age
until they are slaughtered and eaten.
The night following the feast, farmers sit up
all night with family and friends,
recounting stories of sea-dipped pasts
where Coleridge's albatross lingers still,

burdened by the weight of time,
not released until narrative memory fades
into the darkened empty evening
of the passing waves of generations.

Recurring Self

On black chain-link fence sat a gray finch.
Behind it, an empty dog park
Before it, a factory under eternal reconstruction
The finch disappears and the sky's organs play a familiar tune,
calling to mind an apple orchard, glinting sun and
thirsty, high, yellowish autumnal grass

—

The finch appears further up the pedestrian path,
its eyes, a jet-black cathedral stare.
Lukewarm Sumatran roast reinvigorates
a destitute traveler's early morning blues,
shaking off bizarre, half-faced dreams
like a golden retriever divesting the ocean's wet salt
The finch's head twitches and it flies backward
toward the empty dog park

—

On Friday evenings, there were outdoor samba classes.
An enticed crowd watched dancers
laughing and gyrating
to the beat of a thousand drums
Under a patch of earth called home,
it was a tightly enveloped Heideggerian world

—

Sajj and his wife owned a convenience store.
Their *Boston Globe* would be eaten
with Cheerios and coffee, and cat on glass-topped
kitchen table eagerly awaiting end-of-bowl, oat-infused milk.
Occasionally, the gray finch would peer in,
its waiter eyes checking to see if the order
was ready for food that never arrived

—

Evos bar, long-closed, had a rock club room
and a larger room where drink alone sufficed.
Wobbly rebirth nights, with a Donatello painted woman
and friends. Would Guinness's thick lava act as savior?
After midnight flailed its spindly arms,
the bartender placed a towel-covered object onto
the counter. She took off the towel and the caged
gray finch mined the eyes

Merge

Plows of Winchester horses came running from
devolving egg-whites of snow,
shifting wind spilled air northward, leaving a Black Forest.

Vying for the vengeance of good luck, the choir sang zealously,
shaping her nostrils with a three-piece spoon...
nettled was the night!

Yet the dance was still to come!
Emerging from shrouded wings,
was the amygdala pasted white, in the stoic, bloodless ceremony.

Then a needle struck the body, like epinephrine embalmed in
braided licorice. Segueing out nicely upon the border
were the purple scrawls of blood—

The clinic braced for an onslaught
not unlike the Roman Colosseum imploding. But what was to
come? A dose of sequoia leaves enmeshed with a vibrant

birch sapling that was sure to rise beyond an encapsulated canopy?
Or Ohioan mounds geographically raised to a thick shrillness that
would imprint upon the striated skin forever?

   As a man walked down State Street on a brisk morning with
wind raging in from Cubist building gaps, clutching his briefcase
tightly by his side, a woman walked towards him, looking as
though she had read his mind. Though still a distance away, he
noticed her mouth the words, "Are you ok? Is there anything I can
do?" As she walked closer, he noticed her yellowish, cracked
hands bring a cigarette to her mouth and inhale. After inhalation,

she avoided eye contact with the man and incessantly tapped the cigarette in her right hand to truncate imaginary, not-yet-formed ash. As she walked closer, he thought for a second that her nose was an egret's beak and her body, sheathed in a black winter coat from the neck down to lower thighs, seemed amorphous. Walking by each other, an inexplicable thing occurred: whether their elbows had hit, touched or their legs had bumped, some physical interaction was made, and suddenly, without thinking, the man hooked his arm onto hers—she spun around at first making a deprecated face and ready to cry out, yet then her eyes became serious, and she walked with him, arm and arm, at his side. If a passerby or people-watcher had seen them continue walking after this point, it would appear as if one body with four legs continued down State Street towards Boston Harbor. When at the harbor, a cruise boat ticket seller would note that a hermaphrodite wandered past, enraptured in thought.

After Awakening from Briar Patch Dreams

The sky alarms us when gilded by red crescents

There are blasting zones,
where entire portions of cities are made unavailable
and riding by are Vietnamese laundry trains
passing exorbitant days,
with sullen managers who fire employees
if they complain just once.

If one parks near quasar-like, transient zones
leaping out of nowhere,
their car, with equestrian snout and ears,
will be promptly liquidated.
Soporific girls in feline capes that one had seen
decades ago and had forgotten about now reappear
and suggest, innocently, amidst a
vast unraveling into opacity, to go to Chuck e Cheese.

Time is purloined by a vapid beast with
flailing feminine arms and vapid, torpor legs
In this duration, a line of people form
asking questions about the future, such as:
"When will a frothing tea kettle, on a moving monkey's back,
overflow enough to transmute into self-maiming llamas that are
ever engulfing? And in what language

do Uruguayan finches fly to liberation?"

Certainly not the humans! For they're bound by
nettlesome, groping black-ink tree branches of yesterday
and their blood's chemical composition formulated in a
looming cauldron of magnetic thirst!

Even for those who've transcended explicit domains
of purged freedom, there lurk cougar traps
and are haunted by dismal, crestfallen eyelids of sober regret!
Somewhere, under a stale horse's stone hooves,
the impalpable exists...
With every ponderous reflection and sovereign thought,
we march closer—

While seeking, we remain emancipated.

Passport

I.

I was born into these thick reeds
upon emerging from the amorphous, blue-green ocean

As I grew up, with reed marks imprinted on navel,
I went to school, made some friends and had crushes

In teenage years, when my face contorted in the mirror,
reflecting multiple, illuminated countenances,
I donned a bandana from infancy's reed bed

II.

I began traveling to the furthest reaches of the earth,
witnessing the bizarre and confounding—
A man with elephantiasis at the back of a crowded
cafeteria in Singapore's Little India,
Scorned by a man with his kid on a train from Tokyo to Nikko,
who indicated that we'd taken his seat on an empty train,
Stuck on a dead-end train line near Haifa, where apparently
I'd missed the "Akenaba (sp.) Haifa," alert
My friend hugged by a child beggar in Florence
after he handed her two euros,
A father's blistering rebuke of his son in a Prague train terminal,
Sheep fornication jokes hitchhiking in southwest Ireland and also
in Boston's Chinatown with Bengalis ("Lamb ghumabo!"),
Hostility from a Syrian at an Ankara train station for not
understanding his Turkish colleague's
instructions in broken English,

30

A woman's angry gaze from a van passenger seat in Ramallah
after accidentally snapping her picture
when the van rode before my lens

But such othering and seeming radical alterity
was overcome by warm conviviality—
A random middle-aged man in Pendik, Turkey
who'd been chatting with friends but stopped to lead us, by foot,
almost a mile to a bus stop that we couldn't find,
Warm political debates in a Killarney pub
with the bartender that continued hours past closing,
Drinking into the wee hours
with an Israeli colleague in West Jerusalem,
Local neighborhood friendliness to strangers on a back road
Florentine coffee shop where the coffee bar was replete with
people standing and chatting before heading off to work,
Empathy with a West Bank Palestinian
as he pointed to the Separation Wall
and showed us the roundabout difficulties of travel,
Friendship born with a cabbie/business management student as he
sped us across the plains of south-central Turkey
to Cappadocian caves, where Hittite ghosts dreamed of ancient
battles against Ramesses II
Bonhomie at a Bangladeshi American's turmeric ceremony
in a tight underground Harlem venue,
Jokes from Syrian waiters at an Istanbul restaurant—
they had a macabre sense of humor—after telling us they were
from Syria, they held imaginary machine guns,
which they then pretended to shoot

III.

Mollusks riding waves to shore
and cast back out into the sea's depths,
lovers' shade-drawn push-pull,

ever stuck in the reeds' tangle

Freedom's Not Free

Independent Sunshine was stopped by the police
Sunshine asks, "What's the matter, you don't like my freedom?"
to a cop wearing a 'freedom's not free' hat

The cop, timorously, albeit threateningly,
waves an enormous American flag at Sunshine,
as if scaring away foxes from a chicken coop

When Sunshine remarked,
"Thanks for reminding me what country we're in!"
They were promptly arrested for 'violent' defamation

—

Sunshine now sits in the county jail.
When the police tell family and friends
of its truculent defamation,
they nod knowingly

It's no wonder Sunshine didn't make bail!

Sickness

Life, measured in breath-spaces
that light tinsel candles and
shut off as midnight's darkness
caresses pastoral landscapes before
idly tossing them into the sea,
is dimly lit in times when the
body fights, with white blood cell
knight, insurrections taking the
the shape of Viking lances that
carve their initials into the gut.
As the body wars, eyelids cake-up
and the furrowed brow hangs low over
vision, while the eyeball is
rained upon with blood storm,
threatening ocular appendicitis

Where is the self then?

When vision is haunted by a looming
pendulum and the pit every inch
of one's abode? Does it play
dead like a Tower of London raven?
Or does it sleep under
swathes of thick white bandages,
waiting for temporal relief—
when the raven flies out from the
tower and is showered in raining
juniper light, where for a
moment it's not weighed
down by the prisoner's cinder
block cells nor by the torturer's
leering eyes behind dungeon door

Wound

We dress wounds with sparrow wings,
and the wings a vehicle slogging through
a thick, indeterminate jungle where
late 19th-century street lamps illuminate the underground,
while the forest floor is swathed in darkness.
Faces in burial chambers wander past,
evoking the realization that the scenery's
moving and we still

——

We awaken to glinting azure—
the wound sheathed by skin's new layer
and the jungle depleted

The scar: a rabbit hole leading
back to the jungle's writhing tangle

The poem

I.

She ran

The meadow ate her legs
and sky swallowed her limbs
For a while, she was just
a torso looming towards the orange horizon

II.

Irises that couldn't reach the tongue,
stuck in the ear's looping canals
and the nostril's inferior turbinate,
asked the hypothalamus to
drop them into a stew that would
emit a caffeinated sunrise dew,
causing the fingers
to dance on typewriter

It was what she'd thought
In polite and less than a polite company—
her thought-words tattered like
William S. Burroughs' cut-up poetry,
which she kept tightly sealed in boudoir closet

—

Her dream, an inflamed shadow of
cinder block weight,
made her wake up sprinting

bodiless

All For the Best

When jobs went to India or Vietnam,
it was never suggested we be enthused
Instead, the topic was meticulously avoided
until down came the axe

But when AI emerged, threatening to discard employment
like a snotty Kleenex thrown into the gutter,
we're to mime the boss's Dr. Pangloss sentiments.
As algorithms take our place,
please remember—it's all for the best!

Lit Crit

I.

Adjective,
the writer's sapphire
though apostate to
the editor,
who conducts adjectival
ethnic cleansing

The air should be as it is.
Not amorphous,
pollen-replete, warming,
hallucinogenic or stultified.
The person shouldn't be
awe-inspiring, loquacious,
demeaning, exploitative
or a bore.
They should simply fit
into employment application checkboxes—
gay or straight, black,
white or Hispanic.
And they should probably have
tattoos, use drugs or have
interesting sex

Sentences should be short and get to
the point—as encouraged by Microsoft
Word, an aspirational device
meant to transform humanity into
robotic algorithms,
just as the disease-ridden early states
turned hunter-gatherers' mobility
into slavery

II.

But that's just how it is these days.
That's what you and I want,
even we who are ingesters of literature.
Because we will never read the whole
poem or short story if it doesn't
meet certain checkbox criteria or fails to
alight the same reflexive dopaminergic
neurons that blaze fireworks
from Facebook 'likes'
and Twitter retweets.
We want our literature like McDonald's:
a greasy meal for the whole family
that leaves one bloated after eating
and hungry an hour later.

Is this Dostoevsky? Well…Not quite.
It's more a consumptive assortment of words feigning as literature,
loaded with exorbitant amounts of butter, salt and cheese.
Or else, checkbox dreams are realized, bereft of pulse.
It sort of looks like Donald Trump's id: quick, easy, and in a crib.

Dystopia/Collapse

I.

The writing system of Babylon,
new and opportunistic.
The brain of a gibbon,
surpasses the idle hands of dawn.
The dreamer's open lid
exfoliates reality
The puerile yell of the rabble
received a Harvard PhD
The dazed and confused
were the most certain of all

The writing on the wall of Ur,
drunken for grain appropriation
Hunter-gatherers' leisure—
how we yearn for your freedom!

II.

The dreamer's hands were set ajar,
releasing Pandora's scythes,
which chased us each night under tundra moon,
coming closer and closer to dawn's
flailed eyeball that forgot what it
was and is even less sure of what it's become.

The bleached sun stood stooped over the same
horizonal point throughout the day.
Alluvium walls were surpassed by the swelling Nile.
Mud-brick houses on the river's edge morphed,
like Michelangelo's sculpting *The David* in reverse.
Surging floodwaters reached the village's core,
devouring those who remained

Pastoralists welcomed surviving
villagers on the periphery
Often, the villagers would have nightmares
of the dystopia preceding collapse

Ode to Everett-Malden MA

In the near distance, half-hidden behind
a high-rise apartment, is Vegas' upper forehead.
At the very top of the new building,
'Encore' has replaced what was meant to read 'Wynn',
for Steve Wynn, the casino developer, was recently
felled by the MeToo movement for
alleged sexual misconduct.

As I walk, crossing rush hour back roads south through
Everett, I ruminate on a work meeting with the *man,*
who, instead of a deserved promotion, handed me a watering can.
But that's what I deserve—I live on the Everett-Malden line,
didn't go to an ivy league school and career climbing
and networking are absent from blood—
I deserve to live in a city where casinos find residence,
altruistically "lifting the economy."
People in Brookline, Winchester, and Weston
espouse the new casino's benefits,
but how far they keep it from their homes!

Towards Everett, most of the faces I see are Hispanic immigrants,
some walk home from blue-collar work,
and there are mothers rolling their children in strollers
and kids riding bikes. The other way, towards Malden, is more
mixed, Hispanic Americans (mostly nonimmigrants),
Chinese, lower-middle-class blacks and whites and a not small
number of South Asians.

We're essentially all in the same boat.
The wind's lust—which sculpts the waves—
is oceans away

Papa Gino's at closing

A short-haired woman in her mid-30s with a baseball cap on
slides a long, flat, square tray into the rotating oven
and checks to see if a pizza is ready.
She talks with zeal to someone, in detailed
conversation, through a headset.
A community college student working
the late shift complains to his graying, middle-aged male
colleague about previous patrons who took four
Parmesan shakers to their table, "They didn't need
to take four! They really didn't!"
The older man shrugs, uninterested.
An attractive teenage girl, likely a junior or
senior in high school, comes in and asks if her order is
ready. It's not, so she stands by the front counter
to wait. A couple of minutes later, she addresses the
middle-aged man cutting her pizza.
"Do you like my new dress?" she asks, opening up her
coat so that he can see. Feigning indifference, he responds,
"How much did it cost ya?" She doesn't reply, and instead
asks him a minute later, "Rob, could you bring the pizzas out
to my car? It's soooo hot after it comes out of the oven." Silently,
Rob obliges, exiting through the door separating pizza makers
from customers. The high school senior girl starts to follow him
out when her friend, who's simultaneously talking
on the phone to what seems to be a group of guys about
the night's plans, asks if they should hang
out with the guys. The girl in the new dress responds,
"Neah…I don't want to hang with them again tonight."

yeah yeah yeah

Inducted into the regional hall of fame,
her talents were many—
she could write a speech that captivated yawning crowds,
turn sand dollars into gold through hypnosis
and manufacture transgenic humans with
feet atop head—so if ever they were pushed
over, they'd always land on their feet.

But the way she'd zealously say, "yeah, yeah, yeah,"
as though it were one word—"yeahyeahyeah"
was the most compelling.
For this reason alone, the judges would later admit,
she became a hall of famer

A Lick of Spring

A lick of spring temporarily ossifies
winter's thick, nasally curtains.
The clenched palm unravels
like traffic devolving past Dhaka's market town suburbs,
where green and flooded rice paddles
stretch on for *as far as the eye can see*
Teenage boys strut down the sidewalk as only teen boys do
Enthusiastic Spanish accents ricochet through sunsetting air

the smell of the *concealed* emanates
rock salt covers sidewalks

A young black woman walks down Main Street sidewalk on her
phone, "It's been one of those days where…when I get a pizza
later, I'm going to fuck that shit up!"
A Haitian grandmother limps across the street behind her four-
year-old grandson. A white, ruddy-faced, bearded landlord is
waiting on the other side. She tells the grandson to wait up and
then addresses the landlord, "I'm not feeling very good today. I've
just come back to get a few things."
The man does not look happy.
A young white woman lolls on her front steps, chatting on the
phone, "Dude, I've been sitting out here for like an hour, cuz it's
so fuckin' nice out."

Is it spring yet?
No—it's just early February in New England
And the groundhog, as usual, is fucking with us

White Terrorist

I.

Jim Crow wore a wide-brimmed, dust-colored hat
as he rocked back and forth on hot summer porch

When he saw the Feds coming, forcing his kids to
mix with blacks in Little Rock,

he aimed his rifle but did not shoot
Instead, he donned white in the night and had himself a hoot

II.

Years later, his son watched bodegas 'deluge' his town
while sharia threatened to become the law of the land

"Where are ye, my white brothers?" he bellowed into forlorn night
No one answered—they were working double shifts at Walmart

On the Internet, he penned manifestos
that spoke of a flood of the black, brown and hijab

He, as Noah, would build a ship and save everyone
But no one was listening, at least not enough, he thought

He needed to make a mark, make a real difference
So, he grabbed his automatic rifle and set off for deliverance

III.

The dead at the Little Rock unitarian church numbered in the
dozens, mostly children, white and brown.
The cops came, hovered but fired not a shot

From his prison cell, he reckoned he'd made his point,
he would not let the flood tear white America down

Status threat

Plasticized card says:
you belong

Blonde beaches
Irish bars
gray skied smokestacks
shivering winters
damp springs
melted sunrises
purring air

—

People among you walk
with folded lanterns,

loud saris, pulsating fiesta
sound waves, cloaked in hijab,

mangling holy French,
reeking of curry and cologne

—

Drooping Frankish eyes lament—

Things are now different

First Love

I.

With cadence, she devoured a storm
For kicks, he scorched his hair in a campfire

II.

They met at 17 and 20, respectively,
at a time when he gave the finger with eyes and she with hand

He first saw her when she asked him for a ride
through his black Pontiac Bonneville's
open passenger side window,
as it crawled through the crowds
of Boston's posh Newberry Street.
She was adorned with a pink-haired wig,
as she'd shaved her head months before
in a fit of rage, grinning as clumps
of flowing, black hair abandoned her head,
the shaver's buzz snarling
at her mother: "I'll never become like you!"

III.

Their embrace exuded bodylessness,
feeling as at home in the nearly
lifeless universe as a rock, and
Sisyphean boulders disintegrated
as dreams dissolve upon waking

IV.

One day, they went to a Red Sox game
But first he drove her to her a DSS court meeting
and after they drank vodka from a Coke bottle and
she popped some pills as they rode to Fenway
They made it to the sun-scorched, early September,
midday bleachers in the third inning.

Later in the game, when he was returning to their seats after
getting food, he saw her being carried away on a
stretcher and vomiting over the side. Someone in the
hot dog line yelled, "Slut!"

—

Another time they went to one of her acquaintances
to buy pot. After smoking, she went downstairs with
her friend for orange juice. Suddenly, the fullness of the room
eviscerated him and each object's distance
increased rapidly, as though the world
had abruptly boarded a ship that sailed further and
further into the fading horizon or
a tragic movie in which the self is the protagonist where everything
that one knows slowly evanesces. When the seeming eternity
ended and she returned with orange juice,
the earth immediately came back to shore as a hot mass.
He picked up a guitar and played the rest of the silver afternoon

—

Drinking homespun grain alcohol in a park,
they chatted with her friend who recounted
an acid trip where the friend thought she was
being chased by the KKK. When she left,
they idled on swings 'til darkness

—

Once, she gave him tablets of speed:
The floored gas pedal and transcended
speedometer was not enough to
condense highway space into immediacy

—

Towards the end, they sat at an eye doctor's waiting room,
glancing at hanging chads and the blue and
red areas of the U.S. 2000 electoral map in the *Boston Globe*.
Then they went to a KFC drive-thru with her friends,
who gave him their detailed orders
to reiterate to the cashier. When he was supposed to
relay their orders, his mind went blank, and he looked
back to them for a reminder. But, instead, the young women
began shouting things like "I'm having my period!" and
"I'm having a baby" towards the drive-thru speaker

V.

Fall had not quite ended, but they
had emerged
severed
from a magician's top hat

The psychical finger he gave to the world,
which inevitably kept people at bay,
had delivered him a cold, late adolescence,
during which he sat in a scribe-monk's room
enraptured in writing, music and reading,
ensconced in pot smoke, alcohol
and other miscellaneous small-time drugs
After they first kissed in holy Canton kitchen,
next to a moon-glow lake, a flooding wave of
warmth had pervaded his lonely Schopenhauerian soul.

When they broke, the feeling of
womb incubation vanquished.
The world was cold again,
but, perhaps, not as bitter

Marble halls of August

The marble halls of August
And the flowers are beginning to wilt.

She said it was a strange ceremony,
the way they murdered the thief

She said it as though she weren't there
and had observed it as a spectator, from afar

But I smelled her gruel in the festivities' chime
mirroring the ocean in which her eyes swam

I saw her put her hand over her mouth
as if she were hiding all that she'd become

And as the crowd unraveled, she saw God

I saw her take a punch in the face
and it was me but not my hands;
it was just ennui and restlessness

And now when she talks to me,
she rubs the bruises under her eyes
as if they were shoes that she was shining
for a job interview with a strange faceless man
whose countenance she'll color in when the time is right

And I'll still be here,
occasionally remembering her and the first night we met,

when the spring brought the future upon us
with magical dart games and Leonard Cohen's "Hallelujah."

But, I too, will have long let go

Yet those times of rebirth upon first meeting
and other times with holy glow will still recur in my mind—
Like pixie dances whose encore brings endless Lilliputian spears
raining down upon the forgotten earth

From Dhaka to Mawa

Like a caged panther
on sinuous, thin rural backroads,
the SUV adeptly winds
past rickshaws and CNGs,
as though the ghost of Neal
Cassidy was reincarnated
in Bangladesh

——

We had nearly ridden through
the entirety of Dhaka—
from Banani to over the Buriganga
River bridge without hitting
the brakes in the predawn smog-haze
with few cars out and occasional
city workers sweeping the side of the
roads with palm brooms
As we neared Old Dhaka, towards
the south, street vendors
were beginning to set up
their wares for the day

Past the Buriganga, adjacent to
and sometimes winding in and out
of a massive new road construction
project leading to the "soon to be"
constructed Podda ('Padma' in Hindi) River bridge, was
the temporary road upon which we
faced off with trucks, CNGs
and automobiles. They all headed right towards us,
then cut over to their side of the road—
I'd say back into their lane,
but "lane" isn't really applicable here.

To the left, soon after the Buriganga, were
semi-abandoned, half-demolished or half-built
buildings in the distance and a
tightly bound small settlement of
corrugated tin homes in the forefront

The sun rose as a yellow circle depleted of rays,
stolen by the thick morning fog.
As we drove further south—
with highway construction to the right,
upon which were several sleeping hot top trucks,
and to the left were more vaguely-purposed buildings,
sometimes half-finished or half-torn down
interspersed by small rice paddies,
with occasional early morning farmers
paddling in canoes across
flooded rice fields—
it felt almost apocalyptic

In over two hours, we had made it only 30 miles south
to the Mawa fish market
where curious eyes focused in on
one Westerner amidst a group of urban Bengalis
One man followed us, peeking
at me every now and then as though
I had eight heads. Another asked
my wife if I was a foreigner.
She grinned at him and said that
my lightness was due to a skin problem—
we would chuckle about this later!
About a quarter-to-half of the fish displayed
at Mawa lay purposely dying,
to increase their freshness
Some buyers clustered around prized fish, bidding

We walked over a high bank outside the
market, past an area spewed with garbage,
and saw the river Podda,
the main Ganges distributary,
where the other side was hidden in haze and
nine medium-sized wooden fishing boats
were docked at the shore.
Next to one of them, a woman with a sari on
had dunked into the river to bathe
and further down, another woman crouched
low over the holy polluted river to wash clothes.
Further up the river in India,
masses of Hindus would soon
flood the river for Puja

Then we drove through the lush
interior farmlands, beyond the
dense highway side settlements,
where rice paddies, both flooded
and seeded, ran on for mile upon mile—
in Doc Brown's words, "as far as the eye can see!"—
Many homes, wary of the rain season's floods,
were on stilts and most had
thin, raised walkways through the
grass, with pathways leading from the small ridges
surrounding the fields to the paddies below

We headed north back towards Dhaka,
where Cassidy's ghost guided us past
small, dense market towns and
endless bends, avoiding women
in colorful burkas, men with white religious
hats and long white robes and small children
walking alone on the sides of

the road. When he could, our driver
would pass other vehicles, even when CNGs and rickshaws
were not very far up head, but he'd always
step on the gas hard enough to get us
back to our side of the road before the
oncoming traffic could give us
a scratch

Mother Daughter fight

Glass dives off the table,
marrying flesh
Eyes widen

Then another glass,
constructed in a forgotten
Chinese factory is hurled
from hand

The two flying glasses'
trajectories made an X,
each shattering after hitting
wooden tabletop and
splaying out shards,
landing on the mosquito-flooded floor

Afterward, the daughter, temporally "home"
from her new abode overseas,
tore into her mother, the
first hurler, with swords—
"I will kill you when you sleep!"
"Even your old boyfriends cared
more for me than you did!"
"You killed my dad by being
a constant bitch!"

—

And in a dust cloud,
we are in hazy Dhaka in 1992,
where a young, fearless woman with
her daughter raged against society
and its religion. The people, in
turn responded with equal spite—

outside a mosque, on buses that didn't
accommodate the Hindu palate
and in a 'road rage' incident
These traumas would embalm the child's
dreams with fervid nightmare

stimuli
After the mother had swaggeringly
recounted a story of quarreling with
worshippers outside Newmarket
mosque, a laser beam set off
the child's nightmare, and the daughter
woke as a married adult.
She bitterly complained to her mother
of her past rage against society, which had
precipitated flying shards
of glass from the mother's hand

Revolution

I.

The vaulted ceiling opened

rain came down hard on the pilgrims

A crescent moon wallowed
And the Tegeticula moth planted its future

II.

Rock sparrow consumed an alligator

Worshippers, unwedded to horse paralysis,
emerged from gilded woodwork

David melted Goliath in a liquid metal stew

The crowd readied, as though minutemen
set to reenact Tahrir Square

Heads bobbed like storm surfers
in boil's abrupt molecules

The sparrow raised its wings,
gator-breath reminding it
the Bastille could fall
if mirrors no longer quaked with illusion

—

Pilgrims watched rock sparrow morph
into sacred alligator steamroller and
head towards dissolved visions' facade

Hand Held Magic

I.

Distraction, the epicenter of thought-halt,
you drag seared arms in acerbic salt

With ease, shiny vintage automobiles swarm the brow
but downward, eyes are cast, away from unfurling world
to an enticing lava curl

II.

Magic, rabbits pulled from blacktop hats
and Houdini's underwater Charles River escape acts,

has been reduced to ennui…but, low!
As it rests in the palms, it belongs to me!

As with nature and the natives that we've
taken over with gleaming reeds of 'civilization,'
born is an obsessed world-nation!

Now, when someone speaks to us, we hear not
When we pass something in a car, it concerns us not,

(the self-driving automobile will know the way!)
For, we have now transcended the last frontier—that of réalité!

Old City

Jerusalem, city of recurring dreams
How I miss your shrouded morning alleyways,
with sun peppering in through the Old City's façade

Walking in circles, late at night, after briefly interrogated
by Israeli soldiers stationed at two unofficial checkpoints.
With the shops closed and streets empty,
I found it hard to find Hebron Hostel.

I used the city as a place of incubating rest,
while during the day, I'd go on tours
with Green Olive to Ramallah, Bethlehem and
Jericho…some days, I'd leave for the night,
to Akko and Masada—but the Old City,
with warmth amidst contestation, I often dream

Sitting outside the Zion Gate eating Jewish bagels,
swilling Arabic coffee at the Palestinian-owned hostel,
resting outside the Damascus Gate, with tourists, locals and
a reporter mulling over how to depict the city
within a wider narrative of the Palestinian-Israeli conflict

The first day, arriving from Tel Aviv, walking endlessly
around the Old City's perimeter searching for an entrance—
I ended up meandering through a Palestinian
neighborhood, past where the City of David archaeological site
is—
sweating endlessly from the heat and hilled climbs—
Fanta, the savior!
Once inside the Old City,
a Bedouin gave me a brief "tour"
to places I would've likely stumbled upon anyways,
which soon ended at his friend's shop

By the time I left the city, the shopkeepers,
who had often harangued me on the first day and
sometimes drew me into their shop,
no longer paid me any mind—
I had developed the brisk walk amidst the throng:
racing Palestinian children, who I'd walk nearly as fast as,
serious-faced Imams and rabbis
contemplating orations for believers,
Christian Orthodox ministers with long,
black robes and flowing beards,
Christian tourists with
wide cultic eyes of finally
reaching the promised land,
women in hijabs and burqas,
children with long payot…

II.

I took the Sherut early in the morning
through the nearby hills of West Jerusalem's suburbs
to Tel Aviv, where I rode a taxi to Jaffa.
After traversing along a popular waterway walk,
I went into an art gallery and then sat at a bar for a final drink
before leaving for a 5:00 am flight home.
At the bar, the young male and female bartenders were friendly.
"When will you come back?" they asked, and the young women
asked how long I was staying.
When I mentioned that my Bangladeshi girlfriend
was not allowed into the country,
they looked surprised, "But, why?"
I smiled while responding, enjoying the live,
heavily Arab-influenced music.

That night a Peruvian checked me into a Tel Aviv hostel,
where I'd take a two-hour nap before heading to the airport.
He told me of the racism he encountered and his desire to end a
temporary work-study there for Berlin.
At 2 am, I arrived at Ben Gurion airport,
and stood in long, security-intensive lines.

Mint

Her lion eyes' pupils enlarge
Half upside-down, she hisses then coughs
trying to bite my finger

She's not yesterday's weak, horizontal cat,
who, after spewing tufts of hair and intestinal water
from her mouth, lay slothfully on the porch chair

And once she's captured my finger in her mouth,
unlike Kalahari lions, she lets go,
eagerly kicking it away with vibrant legs

Yesterday, we were worried, over twelve hours after puking,
she continued to lay still. Would she not leap again toward the
open door in hopes of chasing sparrows,
only to end up cowering under a driveway car?

Evening came, and with it lingered the day's sultry heat
We sat outside for a bit, sipping beer. In the window looking
out at us, a brown furry face appeared. With half-closed eyes,
she watched us stoically like a Sufi in muraqaba.

The heat drove us back inside, where we heard her
munching and crunching, her face buried in the food bowl.
Then she slowly walked towards us, stretched and yawned,
as though releasing a Sisyphean burden.

Mint was back.

The Crow and the Hog

The hog said to the crow,
"You sit on the fence, looking down into my pen.
But you also see the verdant fields where other livestock graze.
And you fly to the rolling hills, where lurk the coyote
and the fox. Tell me, what have you learned?"

The crow cawed stridently, gloating at the sudden deference of
the pig, who usually had the tendency to mock or charge.
"I see villages, towns and cities, too," the crow began squawking,
"and in these places, there are furless animals who live completely
different lives than you, I, or even the coyote…"

"That's preposterous!" the hog exclaimed.
Then, the hog mused for a moment, "Wait…Are they
like owner Ted and his family?"

"Precisely! However, they live very differently than farmer Ted.
Many of them, especially in the cities, have
no relationships with animals covered with fur or feathers."

The hog's eyes reddened in welling anger,
"That sounds a little anti-animal, don't you think?"

The crow chuckled amidst a loud "Cawwww!"
"Well, I wouldn't say that at all. As a matter of fact, in the cities,
there are some who don't even eat animals."

The hog snorted and blew air out through its lips,
making a flatulent noise, "Of course hairless
animals don't eat other animals! That'd be cannibalism!"

Unable to retain his laughter, the crow muttered,
"But they do, it's true!"

69

Enraged, the pig leapt at the fence where the crow sat,
bellowing out, "You lie! You lie!"

The crow flew off, calling back, "You shall see!
You will soon see!"

"Liar!" the pig yowled back,
before strutting around the perimeter of its pen,
with head held high

Obituaries

Obituaries, how they count and multiple
And the human life so finite in the infinite gold

William Saroyan 1908 to 1981, Jack Kerouac 1922 to 1969,
Gerald Ford 1913 to 2006—even the famous,

who manufactured eternity in seconds, are past and buried!
In youth, while we confronted the

nothingness of death and shuddered with a shivering spine in
parents' empty houses, we also held ourselves to be

immune from old age and worry of the grave.
But as we grow closer to the slow

degeneration that awaits us all, this same nothingness, decay
of flesh and self-vanishing is not a distant fantasy,

but the inevitable magician's door
which will soon open,

leading to the mystery of non-being

Whistle and die

Get old, whistle and die
Our machines are not made
to last the test of time
Breath coarsens, lungs break
heart slow-drips like a rainstorm's end
The night's darkness swoops down
with vulture talons,
tightening the bamboo cage,
and there are no thoughts other than
killing the bird

Get old, whistle and die
Our bodies are not made
to stand for this circus
The acrobat wears an inverted thorn-jacket
The lion tamer a blindfold
and elephants stampede the crowd

Entangled in vulture talons,
the bird patiently waits for dinner
The once illuminated azure
is swathed in brown coffee stains
The spouse is with 'them' and
a fellow torturer
And a walk upstairs is a
three-hour football practice
under August's bleeding hot sun

Get old, whistle and die
What kind of opium will mitigate the pain?
Netflix's escapist vacuums?
The priest's sunny words of a bright tomorrow?
The family's earthly glow of love and genetic perpetuity?
The rationalist's defiant war with God?

72

Morphine's incubating cuddle?

Get old, whistle and die
Here today.

And tomorrow

we shall see

The Gods Return

The rain takes pain
to remind us of its downfall:
gravity's water pellets
cascade onto luminous roofs,
sounding like a termite with
a million cinder block legs

Outside, droplets on skin,
at first isolated then
new liquid skin forms
Clothes slowly dampen
The car ride, a windshield wiper
battle for clarity
Destination reached and
inside the gods' heavy insect legs
barrel down upon roof

There's
a comfort in knowing
that the gods who'd departed
for intergalactic travel
have returned

and gazes exchanged with
passerby confirm that
we're no longer desolate
amidst ice shapes, carving
cathedral spaces on websites
and requesting sunny days
from Alexa

Oh, Wealth!

Intricately designed licorice
garnishes stately walls

The gilded windows wore high heels,
which summoned carrier pigeons
to fly to surgicalized opened skulls
and paint bureaus, cathedrals and nightmare

The crowd outside wondered
what went on in death chamber midnight trap
and licked orifices, illuminated on tv screens,
of paradisal dream enmeshed in honey clove

The queen, with mummified skulls of granddads past,
passed on ciphers to clandestine mousetrap
where tongues are snagged and mangled

The tongueless crowd would now
lick orifices with their eyes

Morning Birds

The birds' parade of incantations
collect the suburb's inhabitants
sleeping amidst a once vast deciduous forest,

Who are all still,
head on a pillow, in the shape of dreams,
returning to the Wampanoag forest
and the North American forest long before humans.

Their songs cradle suburbanites with
a feeding ecstasy alarm clock,
awakening them from post-modern day sleep,
whose dreams have devolved
into Centaurs,
Cyclops and mermaids

Chance

If your island wasn't coughing when I winked
And the steamboat that snored all the way to Alaska
on jovial merry-go-rounds resounding through the
eyes of sound while we die and live again
a million times in an eyelid's breath,

Then surely the unwrapped tinfoil you gave to me on Christmas
And I re-wrapped inside your feast on Eid
would not have made you cough down your food,
sending you to the bathroom where hospitals
would later come, examine you with secret instruments—
behind the curtained word of biopsy—

And there, they found cancer, started chemotherapy
almost immediately—so for six months you had no hair
and could not keep down food—until, oh, a doctor's
error! You are fine. You go home,
take a long nap after an intoxicating, self-induced orgasm,
look into the mirror and smile at the futility of
everything...and yet, in the face of it,
you will continue to subsist...because, if not, then what else?
Die?...
That's for later, when all energy has sapped.

Car Keys

I.

Morning incandescence, disseminating through cornices,
bridges the nude awakening

Transparency lurks amid corrugated maelstroms
Shiva's spheres reclined…
"Where, in all Massasoit's land, are my car keys?"

Isolated from the blood's rhythm and flow of heart—
which gilded road to wrap up in one's shawl?

When in a chain-link fence and betrothed to a collapsed lung,
One ruminates back to one's childhood—
The transcendent elation and gloom;
When upon sunny afternoon, captured was
a monarch butterfly in a playmate's net—
Oh, the anguish! Let's nothing's creature go
into breathing, vibrant blue air!
And, as he lifted his foot to trample
upon the elaborate flying insect,
I knew one thing that mattered more than anything:
Freedom to subsist!

II.

Reaching for rectitude in convoluted junctures,

"Where did I last put my car keys? Hmm. Let me think."
When an elephant's foot is placed atop you, attempting
to diminish an immeasurable soul—
Fight like Frederick Douglass through bleak underground canyons!
Alas, the burden of proof lies in the banquet overhead—
What neurons fire rapidly? How goes the intestines?
Comprehend the elephant beast before
chopping it up for a grand feast!

"I think I know where I left them (the car keys),
if only I remembered how to get there!"

III.

On a sinewy forest road, a cop pulled me over.
When he returned from the cruiser with a ticket, he asked
why I hadn't told him of my abysmal driving record,
I told him to guess. Just guess!
Guess why I don't want my liberty infringed upon.
Take a wild guess!
Liberty infringed upon is death!

"Here they are, goddamn it! Now I can go out
and drive wherever I feel like!"

Mudsill Populist

A mudsill pilot, whose parents found exorbitant wealth,
nosedives at high speeds
and crashes into the clay earth

Everyone assumed the pilot dead but,
like a Phoenix rising from ashes,
he would be reborn as his former self and
ascend as a pilot into the azure

"Truly mercurial," many would remark on his nosedives.
"No one has dared such outrageous feats before!"

In these nosedives, racing through altitude changes at
astounding rates, it was as if within a couple instants,
the pilot had descended forbidden barbed ladders from golf
resorts and world class hotels unto the lubberhead's bayou hovels.
With such dexterity, the pilot could hoodwink the sharecropper
into believing that he was one of them

So that…

So that the ends of happiness are unjoined
So that misery will have company
So that Phoenix won't rise from its ashes
So that Christ will be forgotten
So that the rich will remain affluent
And the poor will stay at the bottom

So that cripples will stay in bed
So that the toothless be distributed bubblegum
So that humans can continue with the 6th extinction
So that Hansel and Gretal will end up in the witch's oven
So that the door may always remain closed

So that the "physics of the impossible"
allows governments to read minds
So that everything may be the same forever
So that there are never any problems
So that speaking is superfluous
So that death is negated
So that souls are thinner than wallpaper

So that we wish we were dead but continue to live
So that we can't differentiate life from death, or
sleeping from dreaming, or fun from boredom

Exclusion

dead bird told to go home
and follow the Tigris
to Anatolian plains
There, it was told,
turn eastward towards Armenia and
head onward to the Eurasian steppe,
where dead birds can fraternize
without looming boulders
waiting to their pound skulls

should they try to cross
invisible lines into spacious
rooms of vaunted crests and
gilded chandeliers, where sit men,
who, with the sleigh of the hand,
can cause livelihoods and
families to be banished to homeless
tents by highway sides
somewhere near the formerly bountiful,
now drained, marshlands of
the southern Mesopotamian alluvium
where the state sucked the life
from Marsh Arabs decades ago

So, a dead bird may think—
is it better to be a corpse
appreciatively fraternizing
on Eurasian steppe than
to live in highway side tent,
where the hum of traffic exiles sleep,
making days ghost-like in
which one haunts the many passersby
with desperate pleas for
silver coins?

Alcoholic Cycle

Where incinerators mince machinery
Where fabled deserts are faced with the axe of ingestion
Where narratives are transformed to quench thirst
Where life is performed within Microsoft Excel columns
Where one continuously strives to keep their seat buckled
but cannot prevent their vision from masticating upon
potential delicious scenery

Where doors are radiators that cannot be opened
and one's skin hypothermic
Where valleys are reminded of salacious nights
under staggering umbrella

—

A cold caught in adolescence can never leave the lungs;
fevers are frequent and inevitable: a self-flaying
cane and cool rain on a humid summer afternoon

Where finally: the delusion that one sip, one drink, one
drunken night seems manageable—
oh, false satori of underworld momentum!
Where the next night occurs and again the same thing happens
The weekend comes, and mountains
have succeeded in the conquest of valleys!
Where the cold winter goes coatless
Where stories are repeated
Where songs are left unfinished and butchered
Where delicious delusional scenery becomes
the suffocating fathom of habituated necessity
Where in more sober moments, one realizes the encapsulating
downward gravitational pull—

but one is now nailed to the Roman executioners' cross
And while crowds around them take notice,
the drink inures from shame

Until their eyes open, they see vultures nearby, licking
their lips—again valleys and deserts inundate dreams.
They again find a house of abstention,
rest their head for a while,
until the vicious cycle repeats

Gaia

Water flows
through sapping
leaves and dangling vines
And the Earth resonates in
deep breaths

And self-sustaining Gaia
folds in upon itself
with corrective breezes
of eternal recurrence

And the repopulation
of Yellowstone with
wolves—who through their
integral bond with the
ecosystem—turn the fallow ground
into verdant lands

And the lawnmower's
moan, calling to mind
lost assembly line Industrial
Age jobs and their
replacement: the bleeding
hum of office building silence
peppered by plodding fingers
on typing keyboard
The lawnmower's scratch on
acoustical chalkboard
is buried under thick leaves
in deep forests of
maple and oak

and an elderly man
delights in charms

and curiosities
of growing old

and a youth
defiantly cackles while
playing chicken on
narrow roads
and then speeds away
from cops

And death, a return to an earth
that vibrates at the seams
with life

About the Author

Peter F. Crowley is a Boston-area author. He works as a Content Specialist/Production Coordinator for a library science company. For fun, he plays in a bluesy rock band around the Boston/NYC area. His writings can be found in Boston Literary Magazine, Mint Press News, Wilderness House Literary Review, Opiate Magazine, Galway Review, Bitchin' Kitsch, Truthout, Visitant, Adelaide Magazine, Ethnic Studies Review, and several other publications. He is currently working on finishing up his first novel that is an amalgam of symbolism, autobiography and subtle cultural critique.